# YOUR BODY - Inside and Out

# Teeth and Hair

Angela Royston

# W
## FRANKLIN WATTS
### LONDON·SYDNEY

First published in 2007 by Franklin Watts

Copyright © Franklin Watts 2007

Franklin Watts
338 Euston Road
London NW1 3BH

Franklin Watts Australia
Level 17/207 Kent Street
Sydney, NSW 2000

Series editor: Sarah Peutrill
Art director: Jonathan Hair
Design: Mo Choy
Illustrations: Ian Thompson
Photographer: Paul Bricknell, unless otherwise credited
Consultant: Peter Riley

Picture credits: Mark Aplet/Shutterstock: 13. Marcin
Balcerzak/Shutterstock: 17t. Alex Bartel/SPL: 11. Andy
Crawford: 5, 9, 12, 19, 24l, 27r. Jaimie Duplass/Shutterstock:
15b. Estelle/Shutterstock: 23b. Vasiliy Koval/Shutterstock: 25.
Edyta Linek/Shutterstock: 28. Paulaphoto/Shutterstock: 23t.
BSIP/SPL: 16. Ray Moller: 11. Eye of Science/SPL: 25, 26, 27l.
Jack Sullivan/Alamy: 29.

Every attempt has been made to clear copyright. Should
there be any inadvertent omission please apply to the
publisher for rectification.

With thanks to our models: Isabella Chang-Ieng, Charlie Pitt,
Kate Polley, Eoin Serle and Marcel Yearwood.

A CIP catalogue record for this book is available from the
British Library.

Dewey number: 612.3'11
ISBN: 978 0 7496 7637 7

Printed in China

Franklin Watts is a division of Hachette Children's Books,
an Hachette Livre UK company.

# Contents

# Looking good

**Teeth and hair** are useful to you and they play a big part in how you look. Your teeth and hair look at their best when they are healthy, not just on the outside but inside, too.

## Eating and talking

You use your teeth to bite into food and to chew it up. You also use them when you speak. It is, for example, very hard to make the sound 'th' without your front teeth.

When this boy ▶ gives a big smile, you can see that his teeth are white and healthy.

## Hair

The hair on your head helps to keep you warm.

There are many different hairstyles to choose from. Some people like to keep their hair short, while others let it grow longer.

▼

# What are teeth made of?

**When you touch** your teeth with your tongue, you can feel that they are hard and mostly smooth. Teeth are made mainly of dentine, which is as hard as bone.

### Hard and strong

Each tooth is covered with a layer of tough enamel that is even harder than dentine. The roots of your teeth hold them firmly in your jawbones.

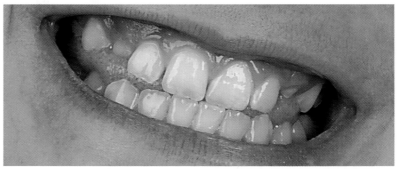

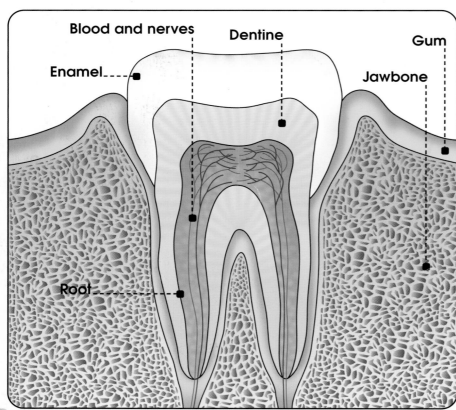

Blood and nerves  Dentine  Gum

Enamel

Jawbone

Root

◄ *The only part of a tooth you can see is the enamel. Your gums protect the roots of your teeth.*

## Soft centre

In the middle of each tooth is a soft mush of blood and nerves. The blood keeps the tooth alive. The nerves tell your brain when something is wrong.

# Long-lasting teeth

Teeth are the toughest and most long-lasting parts of your body. Teeth have been found from people and animals that died thousands of years ago.

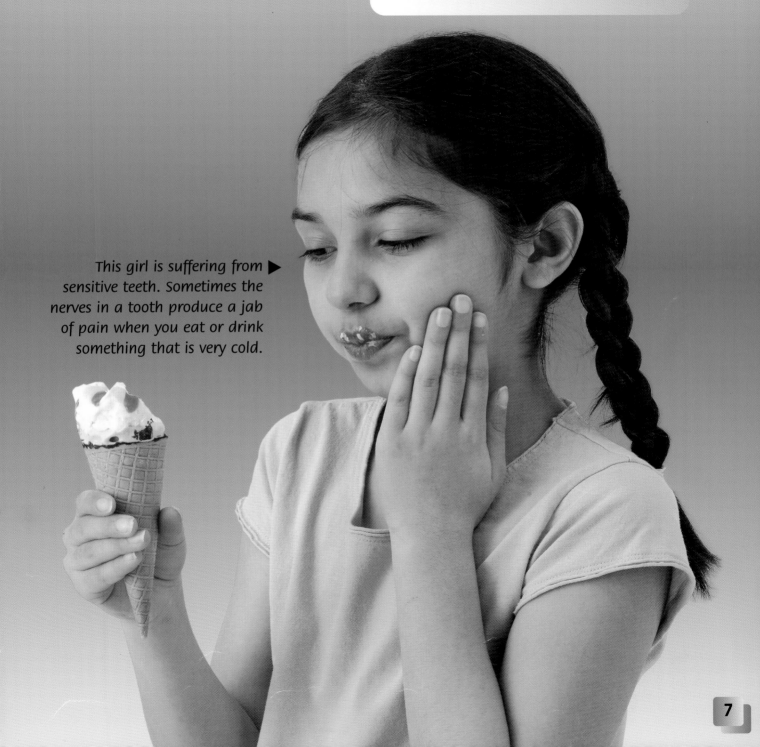

*This girl is suffering from ▶ sensitive teeth. Sometimes the nerves in a tooth produce a jab of pain when you eat or drink something that is very cold.*

# Shapes of teeth

**Your teeth** are different shapes to allow you to bite into food and chew it up into small pieces. As you chew, saliva in your mouth mixes with the food to make it soft and mushy.

## Biting and slicing

The large, flat teeth at the front of your mouth are called incisors. They slice into food. The slightly curved teeth are canines. They grip food and tear off a mouthful.

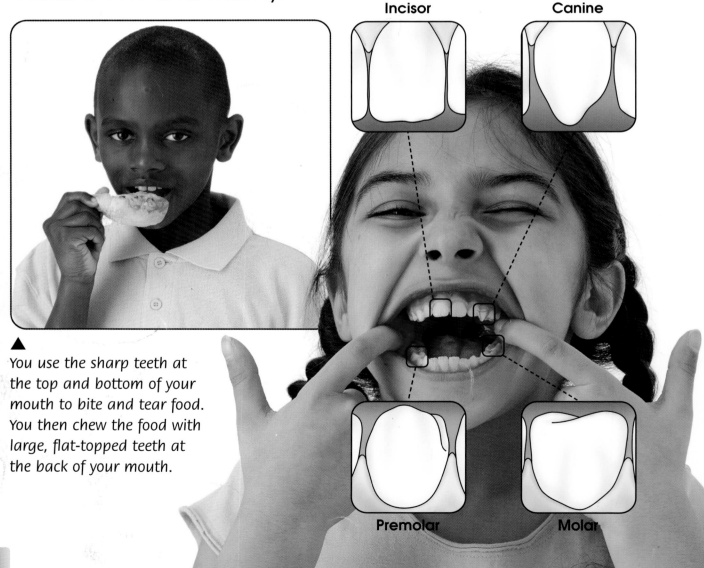

▲
*You use the sharp teeth at the top and bottom of your mouth to bite and tear food. You then chew the food with large, flat-topped teeth at the back of your mouth.*

Incisor

Canine

Premolar

Molar

## Grinding up food

As you chew, the tops of your molars grind together to crush up each mouthful of food. When the food is mushy enough to slide down your throat, you swallow it.

Your tongue and jaws ▶ move the food around your mouth as you chew. This helps the food to mix with the saliva.

▲ Your top and bottom molars fit together to grind up food.

### Try this!

Use a knife and the back of a spoon to cut up an apple and crush granulated sugar. Which do you use for which? That is how your incisors and molars work!

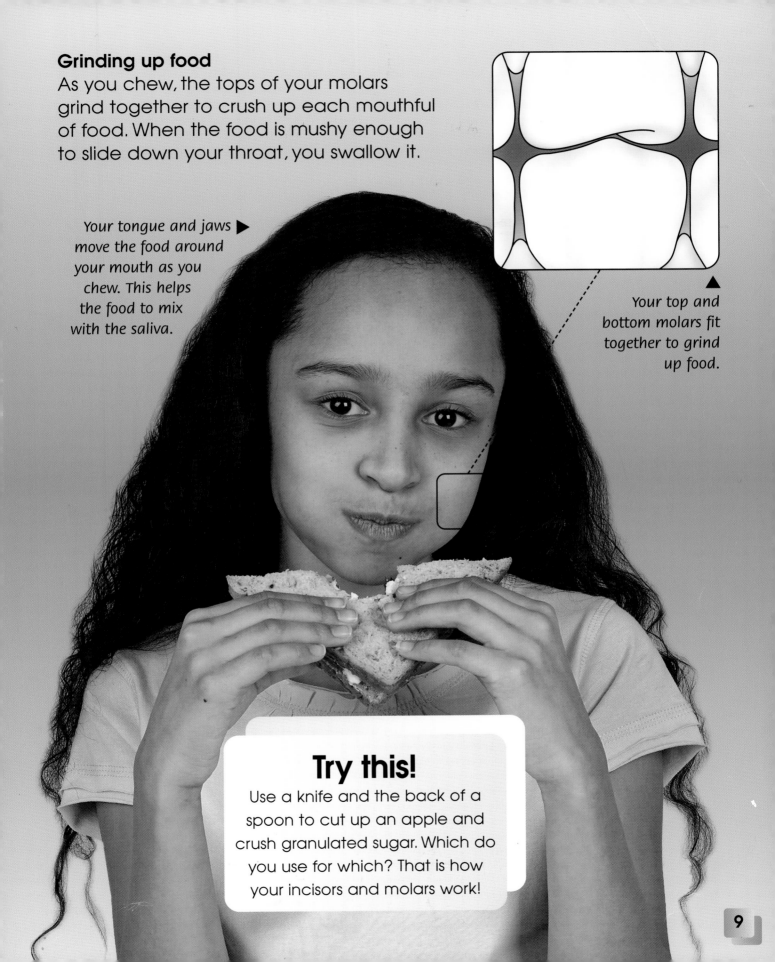

# Two sets of teeth

**When you were born**, you probably had no teeth, at least none that anyone could see. But hidden below your gums, two sets of teeth were already forming.

## Milk teeth

The milk teeth push through the gums between the ages of about six months and three years. The first to appear are usually the front teeth, followed by the back teeth.

◀ *This baby is seven months old and already has a few milk teeth. As the back teeth push through, they make the gum red and sore. This is called teething.*

## Permanent teeth

The permanent teeth form below the roots of the milk teeth. As a permanent tooth grows, the roots of the milk tooth above it begin to shrink and the milk tooth becomes loose.

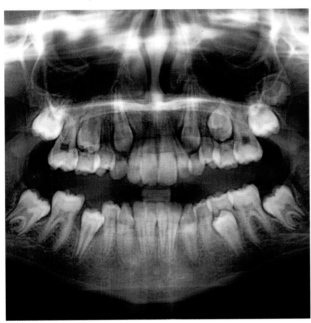

▲
This X-ray shows several permanent teeth beginning to push through the gums. These new teeth have been coloured purple.

## Number crunching

You have 20 milk teeth and 32 permanent teeth. They include four wisdom teeth at the very back of the mouth that do not appear until you are about 18 years old – when you are supposed to be wise!

The milk teeth fall out between the ages of about six and 12 years. First the front teeth and then the back teeth are slowly replaced by permanent teeth.

▼

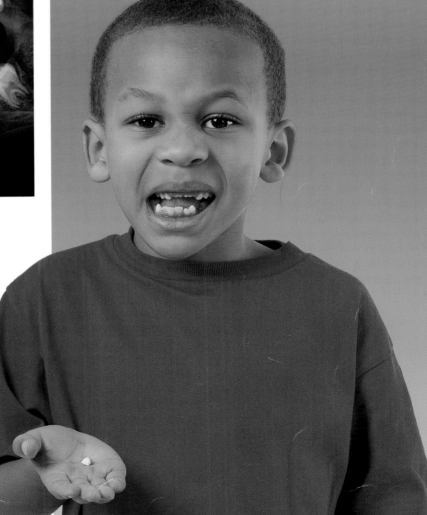

# Cleaning teeth

**If you look** after your teeth and gums, your permanent teeth should last for the rest of your life. You need to clean your teeth carefully at least twice a day.

**Brushing your teeth**
Brush your teeth with toothpaste after your breakfast and before you go to bed. Use a toothbrush with bristles that are still clean and straight.

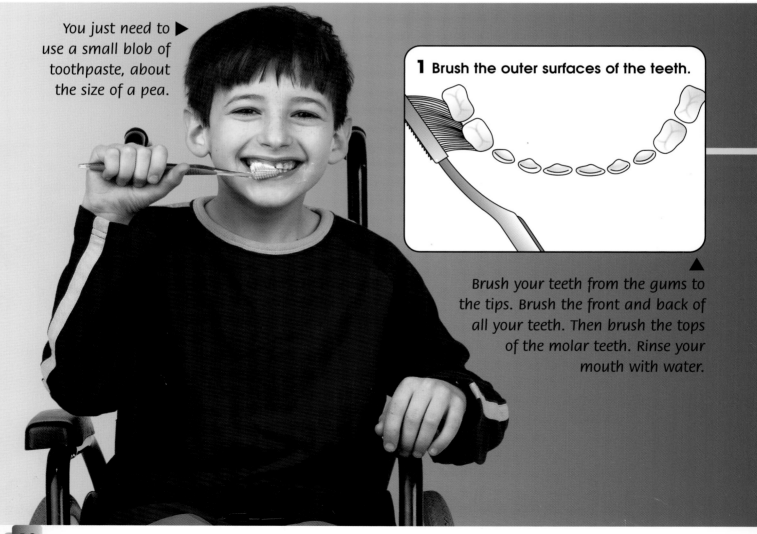

You just need to ▶ use a small blob of toothpaste, about the size of a pea.

**1 Brush the outer surfaces of the teeth.**

▲
Brush your teeth from the gums to the tips. Brush the front and back of all your teeth. Then brush the tops of the molar teeth. Rinse your mouth with water.

## Cleaning between your teeth

Tiny bits of food can get stuck between your teeth and under your gums. If your teeth grow close together, you can use dental floss or an interdens brush to clean between them.

# Try this!

Ask an adult if you may chew a disclosing tablet to check how well you have cleaned your teeth. The coloured stains show where your teeth are not clean. Now brush your teeth until all the colour has gone.

**2** Brush the inner surfaces of the teeth.

**3** Brush the top of the teeth.

*Dental floss is special ▶ thread that you pull up and down between your teeth. It cleans the places that you can't see and your toothbrush can't reach.*

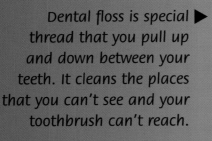

# Stronger and straighter

**The stronger** your teeth are, the longer they are likely to last. The minerals calcium and fluoride make your teeth stronger, particularly while your teeth are still forming.

### Calcium

Calcium makes your bones strong as well as your teeth. You should drink milk or eat food that contains calcium every day. Bread often contains extra calcium.

◄ *These are some foods that contain lots of calcium. Sardines, milk and foods made from milk, such as yoghurt and cheese, contain the most calcium.*

## Fluoride

Fluoride makes the enamel on your teeth extra strong. Most toothpaste contains fluoride to make your teeth stronger. You can also take fluoride as drops or tablets. In some places, however, the drinking water already contains enough fluoride.

## Braces

Some children and adults need to wear braces for a while to make their teeth grow straighter.

*People get used to wearing braces after a week or two.*
▼

▲
*False teeth are specially made to fit a particular person's mouth.*

## Dentures

If you look after your teeth and gums, your teeth should last until old age. However, as people get older, many have to have some of their teeth removed. Then they have false teeth or dentures.

# Tooth decay

**Although your teeth** are hard and strong, they can easily decay and rot. A tooth begins to decay when a hole forms in the enamel that covers the tooth.

## Getting bigger

If tooth decay is not treated, it spreads down into the dentine. Tooth decay only hurts when the hole reaches the nerves in the centre. Then the tooth is extremely painful.

Hole

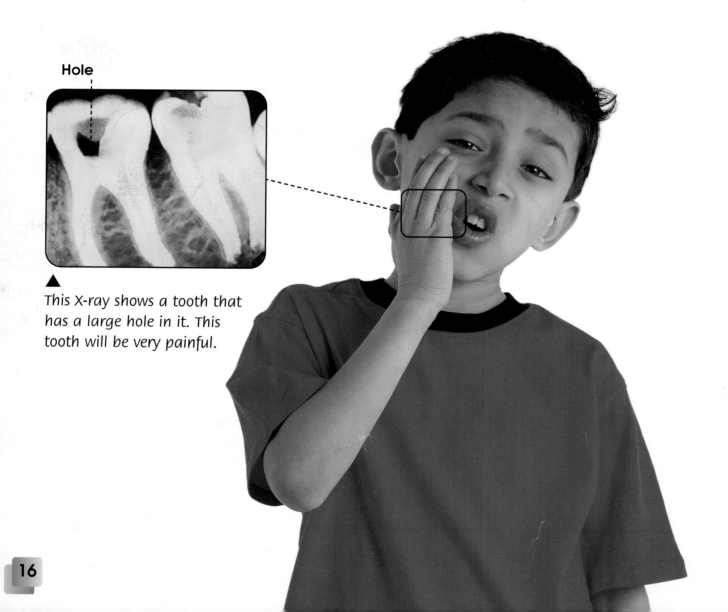

▲ This X-ray shows a tooth that has a large hole in it. This tooth will be very painful.

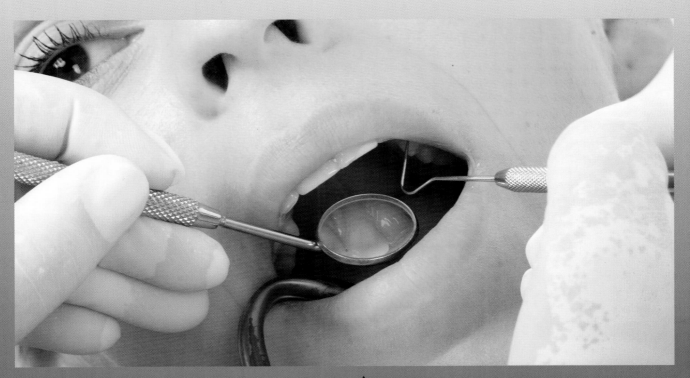

▲ The dentist uses a small mirror to see all around your teeth.

## Checking for tooth decay

You should visit a dentist every six months to have your teeth checked. The dentist checks whether your teeth are healthy and fills any teeth that are decaying.

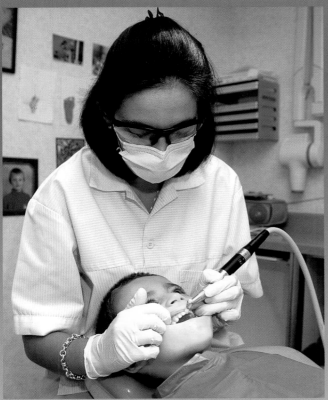

▲ Before the dentist fills a tooth, she drills away all the bits of decayed tooth. This makes the hole bigger! Then she fills it with a mixture of chemicals.

## Try this!

Find a potato with several dark spots, called 'eyes'. Use the end of a potato peeler to dig out all the eyes. Fill the holes with moulding clay. Push the clay down firmly. This is similar to the way a dentist fills a tooth.

# What causes tooth decay?

**Tooth decay** is caused by sugar that clings to your teeth after you have eaten or drunk something sweet. The sugar is turned into acid that attacks your teeth.

## Bacteria in your mouth

Your mouth contains lots of microscopic bacteria. As these bacteria feed on sugar left in your mouth they make acid. The mixture of bacteria and acid forms a sticky paste called plaque.

*These are some snacks that contain a lot of sugar. You should eat or drink sweet snacks only once or twice a day.*
▼

## Mouthwash

When you clean your teeth, you brush away most of the plaque and bacteria. Rinsing your mouth with mouthwash helps to kill any remaining bacteria.

*Have a drink of water after you ▶ have eaten or drunk anything sweet. It helps to wash away any sugar clinging to your teeth.*

## Hidden dangers

Fruit juices, such as apple juice and orange juice, contain a lot of acid. Fruit juices are healthy, but drinking too much of them can damage your teeth. It is better to drink through a straw.

# How hair grows

**Each hair grows** from a hair follicle in your skin. Hair grows on most of your body, except on the palms of your hands and the soles of your feet. It is thickest in your eyebrows and on your scalp.

### Head of hair

Each hair grows for about six years and then falls out. Every day about 30 to 60 hairs fall out. The hair follicles rest for a few months and then new hairs begin to grow.

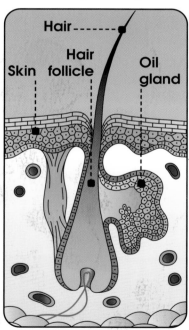

*Hair grows about a centimetre each month. The new hair is made in the hair follicle. The follicle is fed by blood, while oil from the oil gland keeps the hair shiny.*

# What is hair made of?

Hair is made of a substance called keratin – the same substance that your nails and the horns and claws of animals are made of.

## What colour?

You inherit the colour of your hair from your parents. When people grow old, their hair may lose the chemical that colours it. Then it becomes grey or white.

## Straight or curly?

Your hair may be naturally curly, wavy or straight. This depends on the shape of your hair follicles. Some people have their hair curled or straightened at the hairdressers.

*Curly hair grows from flat follicles, wavy hair grows from oval follicles and straight hair grows from round follicles.*
▼

21

# Protecting your skin

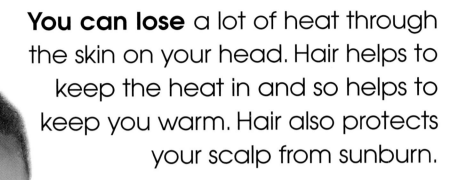

**You can lose** a lot of heat through the skin on your head. Hair helps to keep the heat in and so helps to keep you warm. Hair also protects your scalp from sunburn.

### Body hair

Your arms and legs are covered with fine hairs. When you are cold, tiny muscles make the hairs stand up. The muscles make bumps called goose bumps. The hairs trap air which helps to keep you warm.

## Try this!

The next time you have bare arms and feel cold, look at the hairs on your arm. Are they standing up or lying flat?

◀ Cats, dogs and all mammals have hair that covers their skin. Animals with thick fur stay warm even during cold nights and cold winters. We need to wear clothes to keep us warm as our body hair is not thick enough.

## Losing hair

Some men gradually lose their hair and go bald. This happens when some of their hair follicles stop producing new hairs when the old hairs fall out.

*Some men lose all their hair, while others* ▶
*lose just some of it, or none at all.*

### Sunscreen

When the Sun is strong the hair on your body is not thick enough to protect your skin from sunburn. You should cover your skin and use suncream to protect yourself.

◀ *A sunhat protects your face and neck from sunburn. People with very short hair, or no hair, must wear a hat or cap in the Sun to protect their scalps, too.*

# Looking after hair

**Keeping your hair** tidy and clean helps to keep it healthy. Brushing or combing your hair stops it getting tangled.

## Washing your hair

You should wash your hair about twice a week. Washing your hair also washes your scalp. When you have shampooed your hair, rinse it well to wash out all the soap.

◀ Brush or comb your hair when you get up in the morning.

If your hair is dry you may need to use a hair conditioner after washing it. The conditioner makes your hair sleek and smooth. ▼

## Natural conditioner

Each hair makes its own oil and conditions itself. People have dry hair when their hair glands (see page 20) do not make enough oil. People whose hair makes too much oil, have oily hair.

## Haircuts

A haircut gives you a particular hairstyle and keeps your hair looking neat. If you have long hair, you should have the ends cut occasionally.

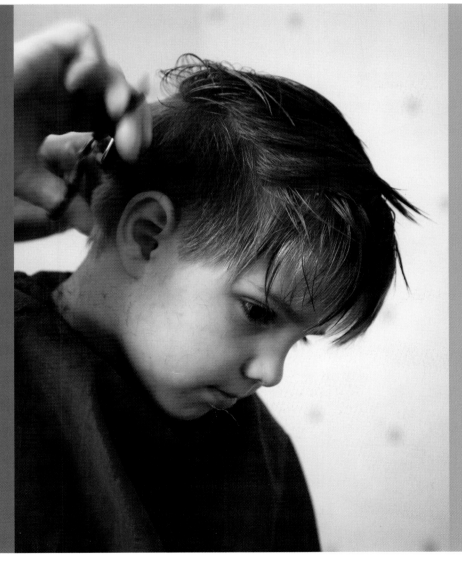

▲
*Sometimes the ends of your hair split. This is what a split end looks like under a microscope.*

◀ *A haircut gets rid of split ends.*

# Head lice

**Head lice** are tiny insects that live in your hair. Head lice are hard to spot because they move through your hair very fast. You know you have them when they make your head itch.

## Catching head lice

You catch head lice when your hair touches the hair of someone who already has them. The head lice move quickly from one person's head to another's.

*This head louse is shown under a microscope. A head louse feeds by biting your scalp and sucking your blood. The bites can become very itchy – they make you scratch!*

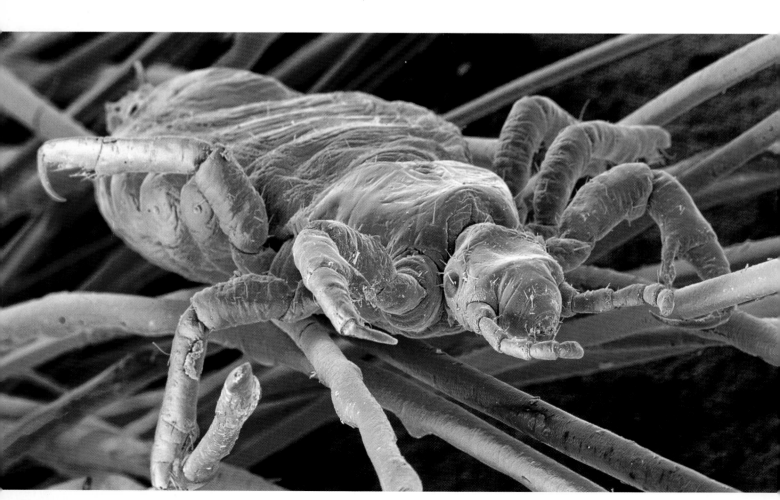

## Nits

Head lice lay many tiny eggs. The eggs are called 'nits' and each one is glued to a different hair. When they hatch, the empty eggs stay stuck to the hairs.

▲

*It is easier to spot nits in your hair than head lice. Good places to look are in the hair behind your ears and at the back of your neck.*

# Dandruff

Don't confuse dandruff and nits! Dandruff is flakes of skin from your scalp. You can easily shake them from your hair. You can't get rid of nits by shaking or brushing your hair.

*Head lice are only one of the things that can make your scalp itchy. A dry scalp, dirty hair and dandruff can also make your head itch.*

▼

# Treating head lice

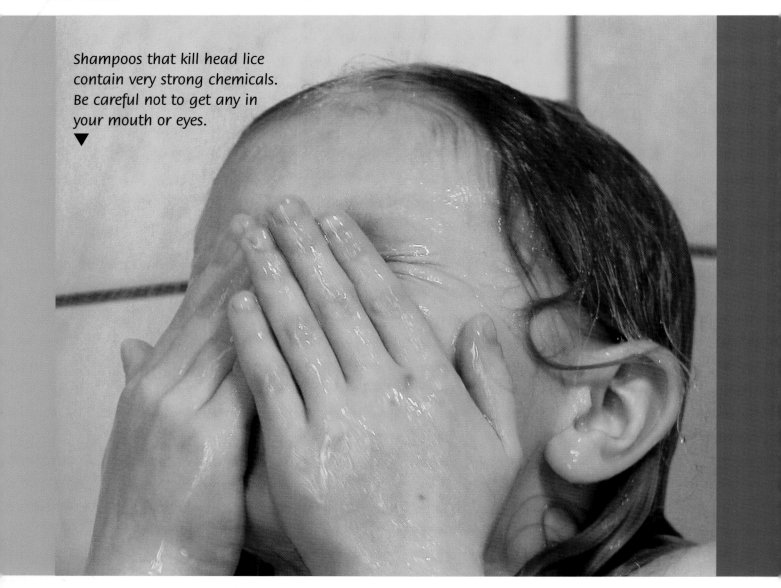

Shampoos that kill head lice contain very strong chemicals. Be careful not to get any in your mouth or eyes. ▼

**Ordinary shampoo** does not kill head lice, so you have to use a special shampoo. In case any nits survive, you have to use the shampoo again two weeks later.

**Special shampoo**
Head lice pass very easily from one person to another. If one person in a family is infected, the whole family has to use the special shampoo.

## Try this!

Sometimes head lice are not killed by special shampoos. Another way to kill lice is to comb olive oil through your hair and leave it overnight. The oil suffocates the lice and you can comb them out the next day.

## Nit combs

When you have rinsed out the shampoo, comb your hair with a special nit comb. This will comb out any dead lice and nits left in your hair. Using conditioner makes it easier to comb.

*Head lice cannot move* ▶ *quickly through wet hair. After you wash your hair, comb it with a nit comb to catch any lice that are in your hair.*

29

# Glossary

**acid**
A liquid that can make holes in solid things.

**bacteria**
Tiny living things that are too small to see except through a microscope.

**calcium**
A substance found in some foods that makes your teeth and bones strong.

**canines**
Four sharp, pointed teeth that you use to grip food.

**chemicals**
Substances that things are made from.

**dandruff**
When the scalp becomes dry and sheds small flakes of dead skin.

**decay**
To rot or to begin to rot.

**dentine**
A hard substance that forms most of each tooth.

**disclosing tablet**
A tablet that colours plaque on your teeth when you suck it.

**enamel**
A hard, shiny substance that covers each tooth.

**fluoride**
A substance that makes your teeth less likely to decay.

**hair conditioner**
A creamy liquid that you put on wet hair to make it less dry and more shiny.

**hair follicle**
A small hollow in the skin from which a hair grows.

**incisors**
Large flat teeth at the front of the mouth.

**infected**
Having caught something, such as head lice or an illness.

**jawbone**
Bone inside your mouth that holds your teeth.

**keratin**
The hard substance that hair and nails are made of.

**microscopic**
So small it can only be seen through a microscope.

**molars**
Big, wide teeth at the back of your mouth.

**nerves**
Tiny strands that carry messages to and from the brain.

**nit comb**
A small comb with the teeth very close together which can remove nits and head lice from the hair.

**plaque**
A sticky paste made by bacteria that causes tooth decay.

**saliva**
A liquid that is made inside your mouth.

**suffocate**
To kill something by stopping it breathing.

**wisdom teeth**
Four large teeth that come through when you are about 18 or older at the very back of your mouth.

## FURTHER INFORMATION
## WEBSITES
*www.bbc.co.uk/science/ humanbody/body* gives you games and interactive information about the human body.

*www.kidshealth.org/kid/ stay_healthy/body/teeth.html* gives you information about your teeth and how to clean them.

*www.kidshealth.org/kid/ill_injure/ sick/lice.html* tells you about head lice and how to get rid of them.

# Index

These are the lists of contents for each title in *Your Body - Inside and Out*

**Bones and Muscles**
Under your skin • Your skeleton • Body armour • Joints • Fingers and thumbs • Shoulders and hips • Your neck • Your spine • Muscles move your bones • Moving your elbow • Exercise • Moving your face • Breaks and sprains

**Food and Digestion**
Food is fuel • Energy foods: starches • Energy foods: sugars • Body-building foods • Fats and oils • Fruit and vegetables • What happens to food? • Chew and swallow • Into the intestines • Absorbing food • Water and waste • Problems with foods • A healthy diet

**Growing**
The cycle of life • Producing babies • Inside the womb • Everyone is different • A newborn baby • From six months to one year old • Toddlers • From toddler to child • Young children • From child to adult • Fully grown • Getting older • Keeping healthy

**Heart and Lungs**
The heart and lungs • The heart is a muscle • The heart is a pump • What is blood for? • We need oxygen • Your ribs move • Lungs are sponges • Gases in and out • The blood system • The four-part heart • A healthy heart • Strong heart and lungs • Checking your pulse

**Senses**
What are the senses? • Your brain • Seeing • Inside the eye • Wearing glasses • Hearing • Inside your eye • Hard of hearing • Smelling • Tasting • Touching • Heat and pain • Working together

**Teeth and Hair**
Looking good • What are teeth made of? • Shapes of teeth • Two sets of teeth • Cleaning teeth • Stronger and straighter • Tooth decay • What causes tooth decay? • How hair grows • Protecting your skin • Looking after hair • Head lice • Treating head lice